Color your way through the alphabet

A is for APPLE,
so shiny and red,
A crunchy
delight that
keeps us well-
fed.

A a

B is for BALL,
we toss and we
play.
Bouncing around in
the park every day.

B b

C is for CAT, with its fur soft and sleek.

It purrs and meows, what a sweet little sneak.

C c

D is for DOG, our loyal best friend, With a wag of its tail, fun never ends.

D d

E is for
ELEPHANT, big and
so grand,
With a trunk and
large ears, it roams
through the land.

E e

F is for FISH,
swimming in the
sea,
With scales that
shimmer, they glide
gracefully.

F f

G is for GIRAFFE ,
tall and so proud,
With a neck long
and high, it stands
out in a crowd.

G g

H is for HAT worn
on our head,
To keep us warm
and stylishly led.

H h

I is for IGLOO,
made out of snow,
A cozy icehouse in
the Arctic's glow.

I i

J is for
JELLY, wobbly and
sweet,
A colorful treat
that's fun to eat.

J j

K is for KITE,

soaring so high,

It dances with the

wind up in the sky.

K k

L is for LION, the jungle's great king, With a mighty roar, it makes the forest sing.

M is for MONKEY ,
swinging in trees,
Chattering and
laughing, so full of
glee.

M m

N is for NEST ,

where baby birds

sleep,

In a cozy home

high, secrets they

keep.

N n

O is for Octopus,
with eight wavy
arms,
A sea creature
that charms with
its underwater
charms.

P is for Penguin,
waddling around,
In icy cold lands,
where their friends
can be found.

P p

Q is for Queen,
with a crown on her
head,
In a castle she lives,
where she's royally
led.

Q q

R is for Rainbow, a colorful sight,
After rain showers, it's a bright light.

R r

S is for Star,

twinkling at night,

High up in the sky,

shining so bright.

S s

T is for Train, on tracks it goes, With a choo-choo sound, and a whistle that blows.

T t

U is for Umbrella,

on rainy days,

It keeps us dry in

so many ways.

U u

V is for Violin, with strings that sing, Making beautiful music, such a lovely thing.

V v

W is for Whale, enormous and grand, Swimming through oceans, a sight so grand.

W w

X is for Xylophone, with bars to play, A musical instrument, brightening our day.

X x

Y is for Yak, with fur thick and warm, It roams in the mountains, safe from the storm.

Y y _____

Z is for Zebra,

with stripes black

and white,

Galloping in fields,

a wonderful sight.

Z z

From A to Z, we've

learned so much,

About animals, objects,

and the world as such.

Letters are fun, as

you can see,

They help us read and

write with glee!

Made in the USA
Las Vegas, NV
29 November 2024

12854733R00031